ABC
All-American Riddles

written by
Mara & Ford Smith

illustrated by
Jennifer Johnson Haywood

Peel Productions, Inc.
COLUMBUS, NC

Published by Peel Productions, Inc.
PO Box 546, Columbus NC 28722
www.peelbooks.com

Printed in China

Library of Congress Cataloging-in-Publication Data

Smith, Mary Helen.
  ABC all-American riddles / written by Mara & Ford Smith ;
illustrated by Jennifer Johnson Haywood.
     p. cm.
  "ABC riddles book."
  ISBN 0-939217-56-2 (alk. paper)
1. United States--History--Juvenile literature. 2. Riddles,
American--Juvenile literature. I. Smith, Shuford. II. Haywood,
Jennifer Johnson. III. Title.

  E178.3.S646 2004
  973--dc22

                          2004011670

*To our aunts, Alice and Betty,
who have loved children and poetry.*
                                    MS & FS

*To all the men and women of our
military who put our country before
their own lives each and every day.*
                                    JJH

a_ _ _ _ _

My name has five letters. It starts with an A.
A kind man named Johnny gave my seeds away.
A computer of fame
and New York City use my name.
Delicious pies are made from me.
Can you guess? What can I be?

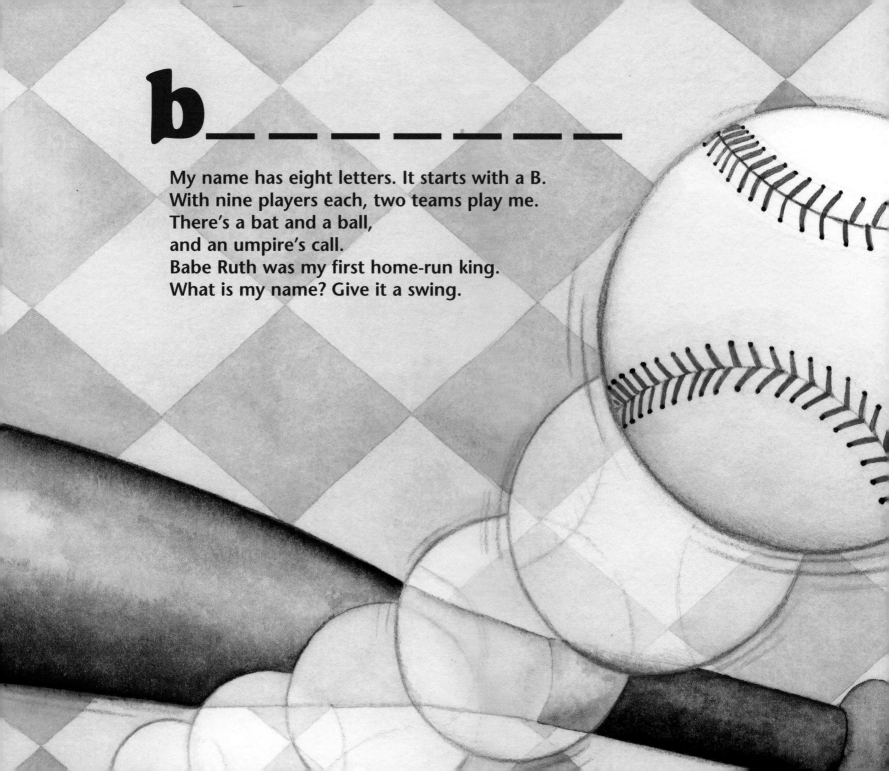

b_ _ _ _ _ _ _

My name has eight letters. It starts with a B.
With nine players each, two teams play me.
There's a bat and a ball,
and an umpire's call.
Babe Ruth was my first home-run king.
What is my name? Give it a swing.

c_ _ _ _ _l

My name starts with C and ends with an L.
I am a building and a symbol as well.
Members of Congress call me home.
My big top is a great, white dome.
I stand tall in Washington, D.C.
What am I? Can you name me?

D _ _ _ _ _ _

A famous cartoonist, my name starts with D.
My characters are stars in movies and TV.
Of all the stars I've created,
Mickey is most celebrated.
Magical kingdoms are named for me.
My first name is Walt. Who can I be?

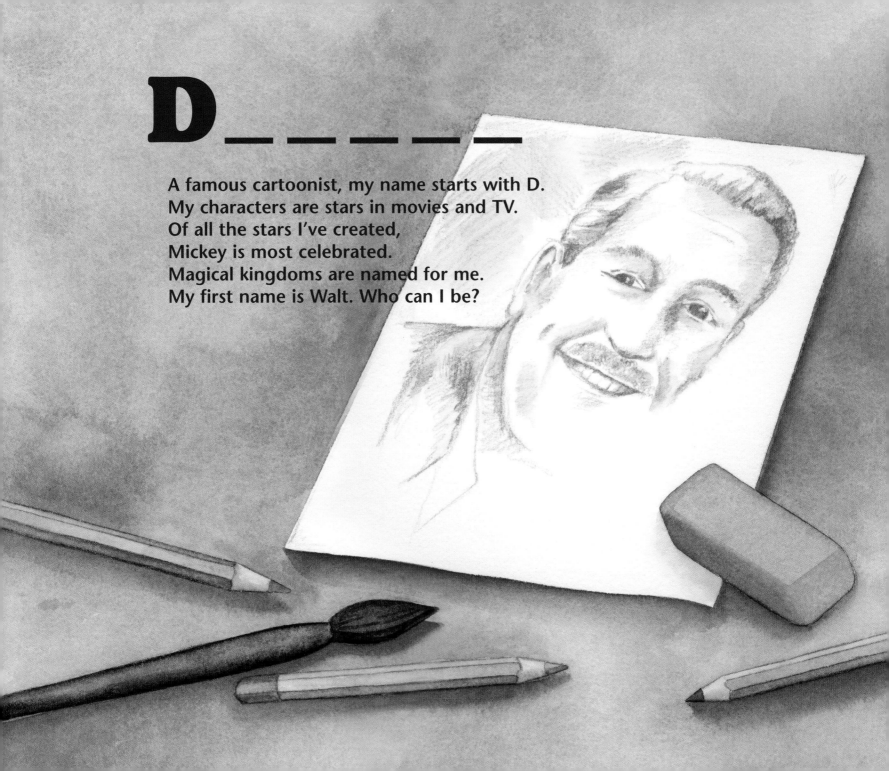

e_ _ _ _

E starts my name. I'm a large bird of prey.
I'm also a symbol of the U.S.A.
In treetops I nest
and perch to rest.
I am your national bird.
What's my name? Say the word.

f _ _ _

F starts my name. It's four letters wide.
Americans respect and salute me with pride.
Above schools I fly.
In parades I'm held high.
Stars and stripes are part of me.
Can you guess? Oh, say can you see?

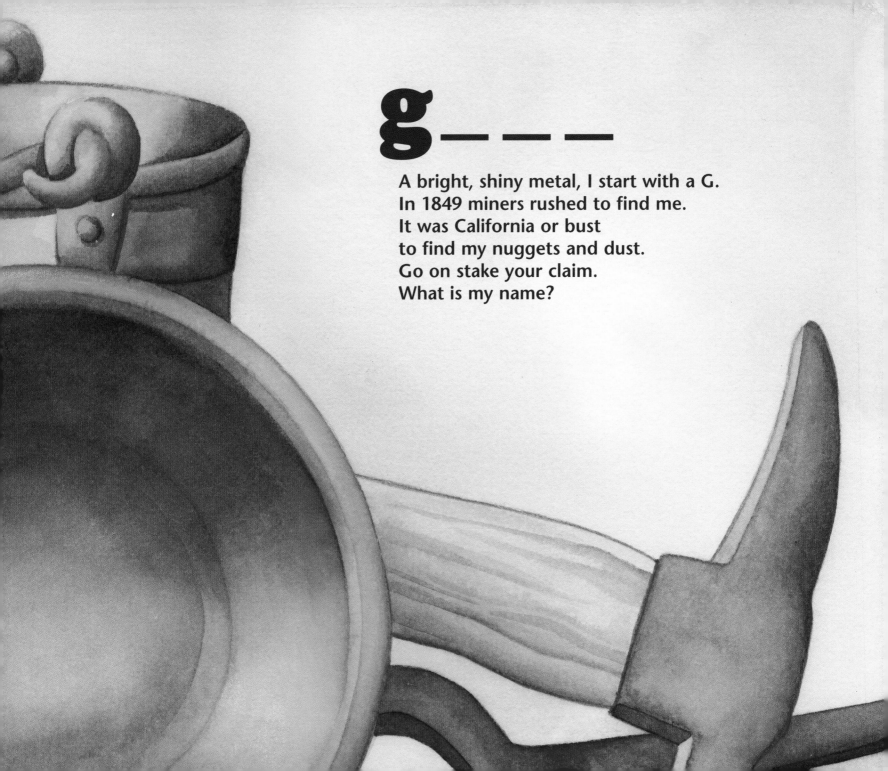

g— — —

A bright, shiny metal, I start with a G.
In 1849 miners rushed to find me.
It was California or bust
to find my nuggets and dust.
Go on stake your claim.
What is my name?

H _ _ _ _ _ i

My name starts with H and ends with an I.
I have mountains, volcanoes, and beaches close by.
Grass skirts and flower leis
invite you for holidays.
My hula dance is great to see.
I'm the 50th state. Can you name me?

I _ _ _ _ _ _

Our name begins with I. It's seven letters long.
As native Americans, to tribes we belong.
Because of white man's fears,
we walked the Trail of Tears.
Find us in cities and on reservations too.
Do you know our common name?
Can you guess who?

j _ _ _

A four letter word, I begin with a J.
I'm often played in a lively way.
Trumpets, sax, and drums combine
to make my special sound divine.
I'm as American as music can be.
What am I called? Can you name me?

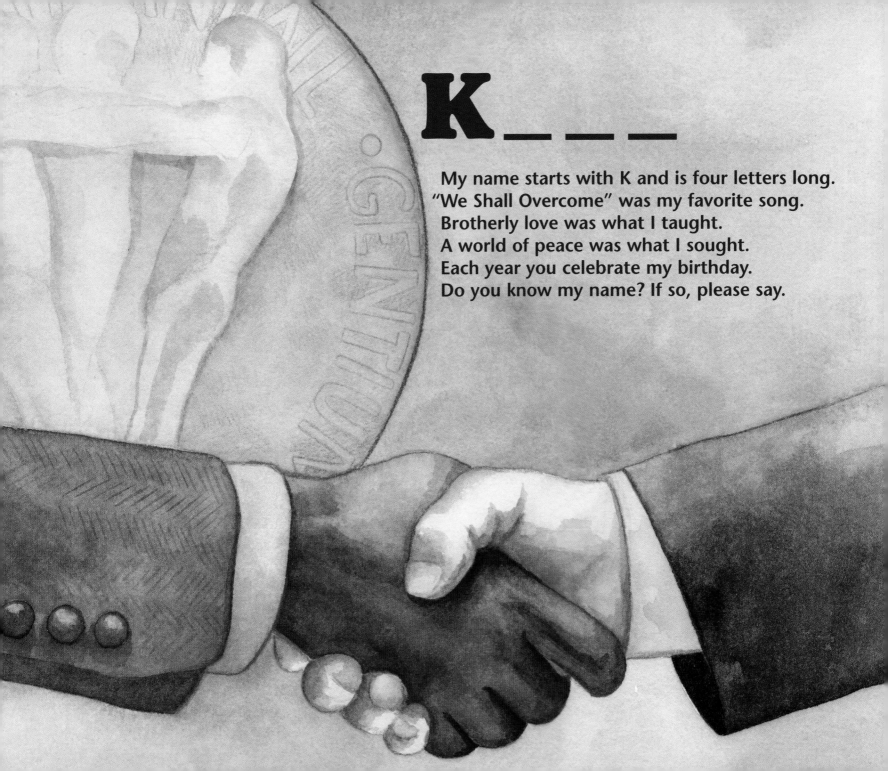

K _ _ _

My name starts with K and is four letters long.
"We Shall Overcome" was my favorite song.
Brotherly love was what I taught.
A world of peace was what I sought.
Each year you celebrate my birthday.
Do you know my name? If so, please say.

1 — — — — — — — — — — —

I stand for freedom and begin with an L.
In 1776, there was a ringing of my bell.
A national island of fame
has a statue with my name.
I want all people to be free.
Who or what can I be?

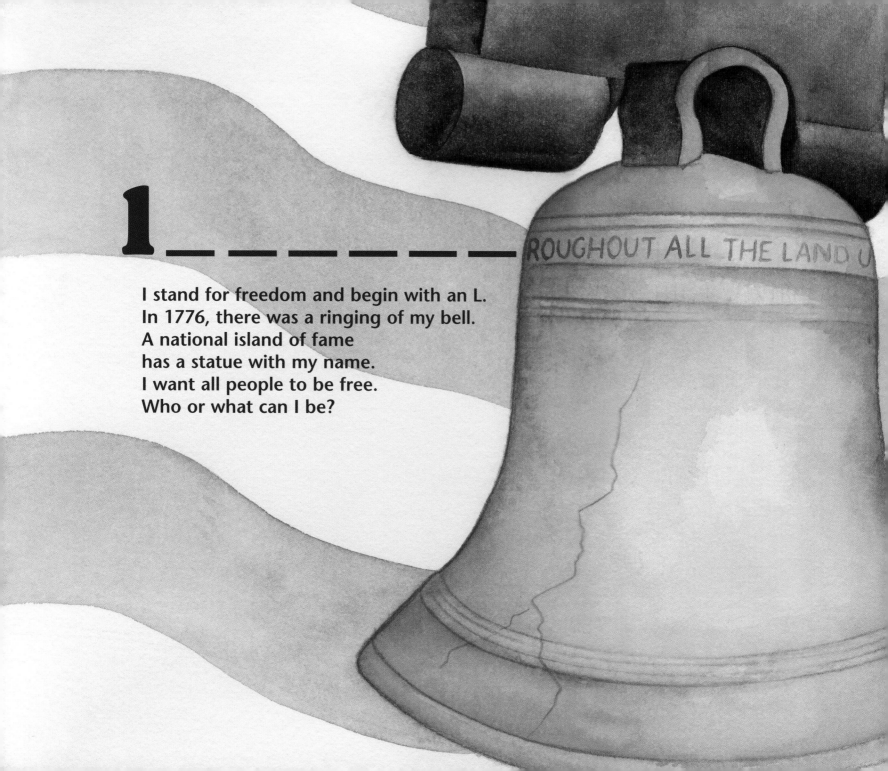

ROUGHOUT ALL THE LAND U

m_ _ _ _ _ _ y

My name starts with M and ends with Y.
Mighty and strong, on me you rely.
On air, sea, or land,
in uniforms grand,
I'm ready to go.
What am I? Do you know?

N＿＿A

My name starts with N and ends with an A.
Scientists work and explore here each day.
They research the stars,
put a robot on Mars,
and send spaceships faraway.
What am I? Can you say?

O_ _

A natural resource, I start with an O.
A thick greasy liquid, I make machines go.
Big rigs drill for me
under ground, under sea.
When I burn, I spark or flame.
Don't slip up. What's my name?

P_ _ _ _ _ _ _ _

P begins our unusual name.
Years ago, from England we came.
We sailed the Mayflower across the sea.
On Plymouth we landed to be free.
Natives helped us a great deal.
To give our thanks, we cooked a meal.
We shared the first Thanksgiving Day.
What is our name? Can you say?

Q _ _ _ k _ _

My name starts with Q. There's also a K.
I live and dress in a simple way.
As a "Friend," I'm against all war.
I think that peace can give us more.
On my word you can rely.
Can you guess? What am I?

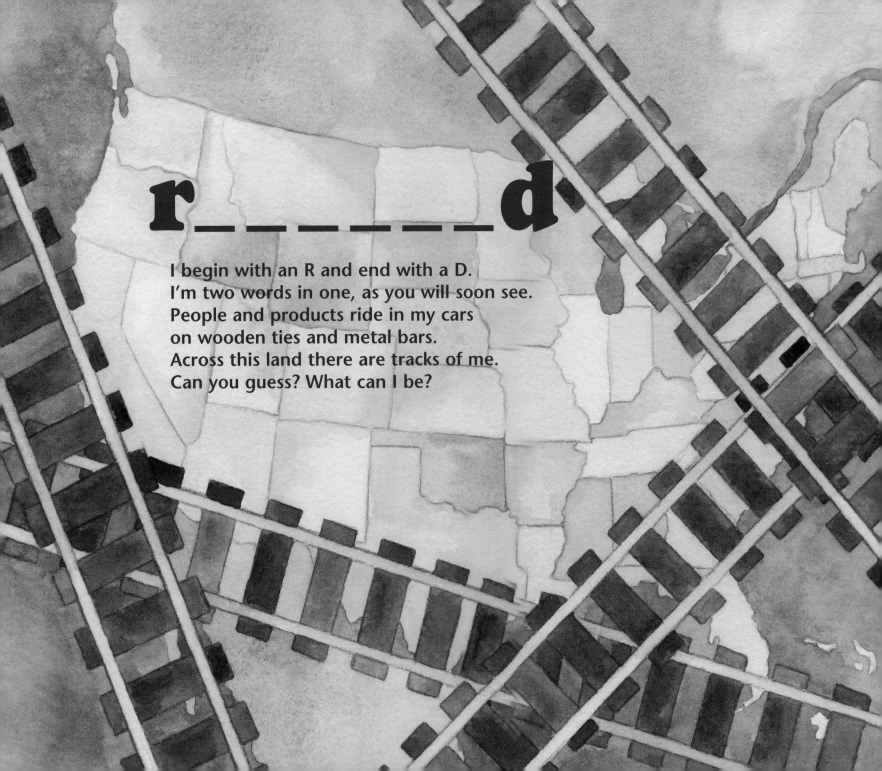

r_____d

I begin with an R and end with a D.
I'm two words in one, as you will soon see.
People and products ride in my cars
on wooden ties and metal bars.
Across this land there are tracks of me.
Can you guess? What can I be?

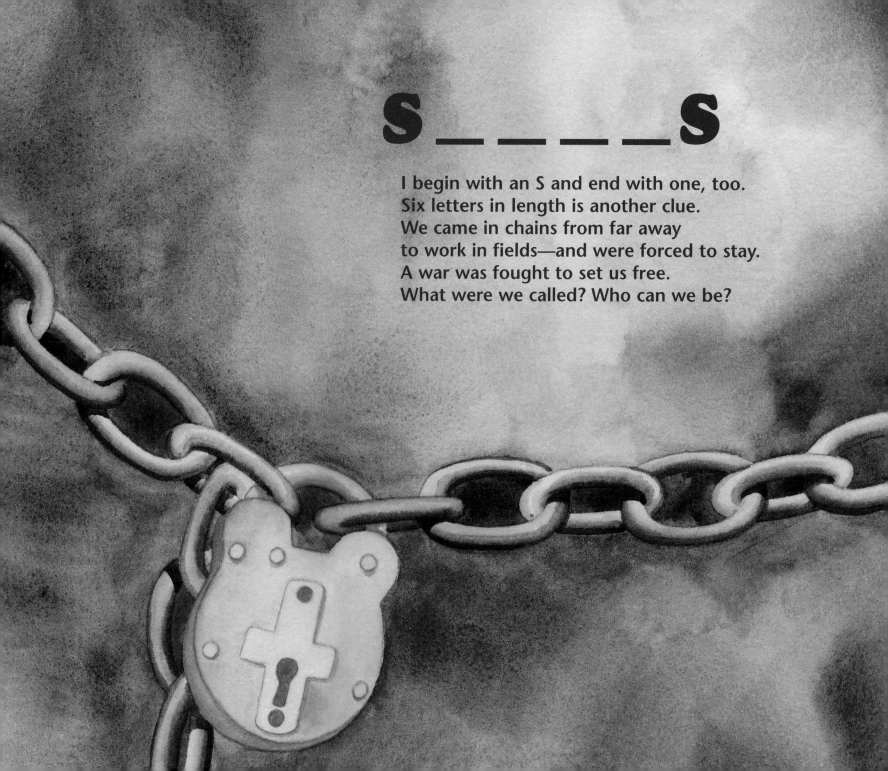

S _ _ _ _ S

I begin with an S and end with one, too.
Six letters in length is another clue.
We came in chains from far away
to work in fields—and were forced to stay.
A war was fought to set us free.
What were we called? Who can we be?

t_____n

My name ends with N, but starts with a T.
Most American homes have at least one of me.
I'm something you see and hear over distance—
a movie, a cartoon, the news, for instance.
You can watch commercials on me.
Oh what can I possibly be?

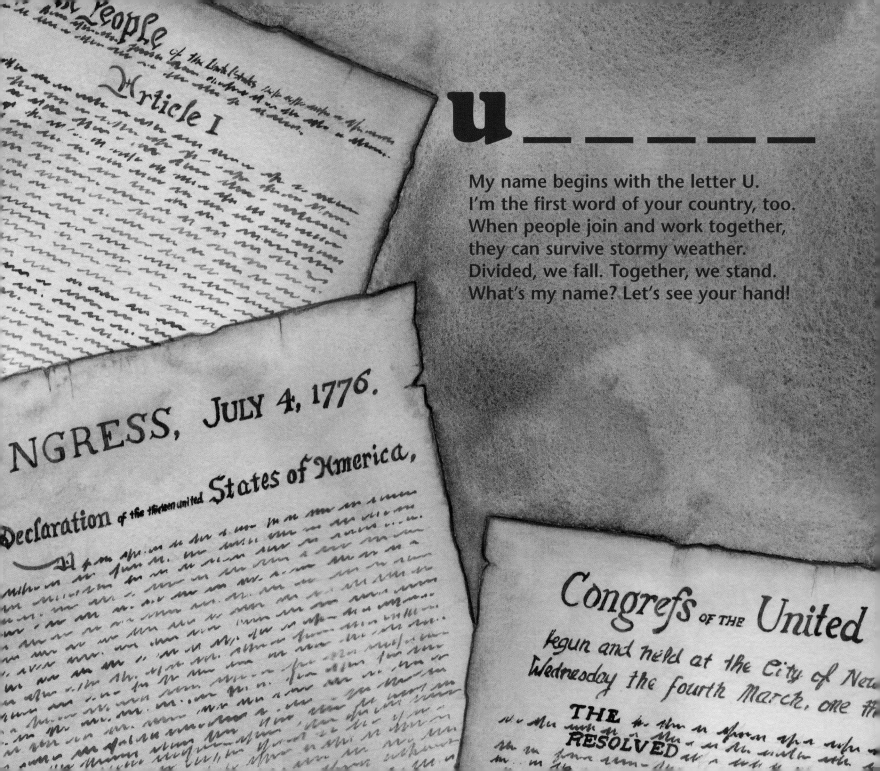

u_ _ _ _ _ _

My name begins with the letter U.
I'm the first word of your country, too.
When people join and work together,
they can survive stormy weather.
Divided, we fall. Together, we stand.
What's my name? Let's see your hand!

v_ _ e

I start with a V and end with an E.
I'm a choice you make like 1, 2, or 3.
In any election,
you make your selection,
by making a mark or raising your hand.
What is my name? Go on, take your stand!

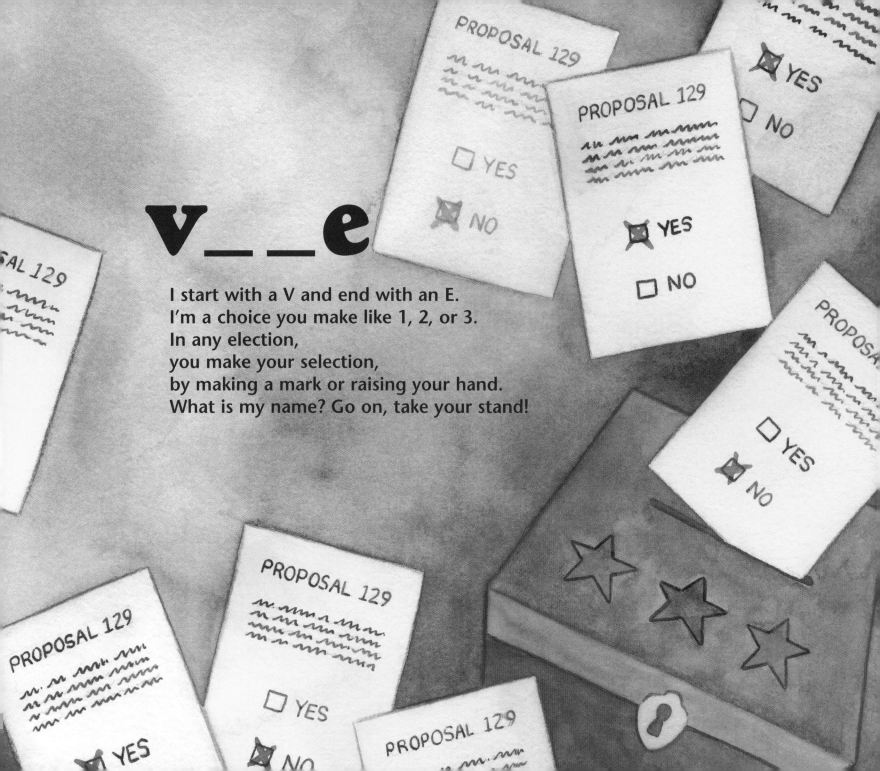

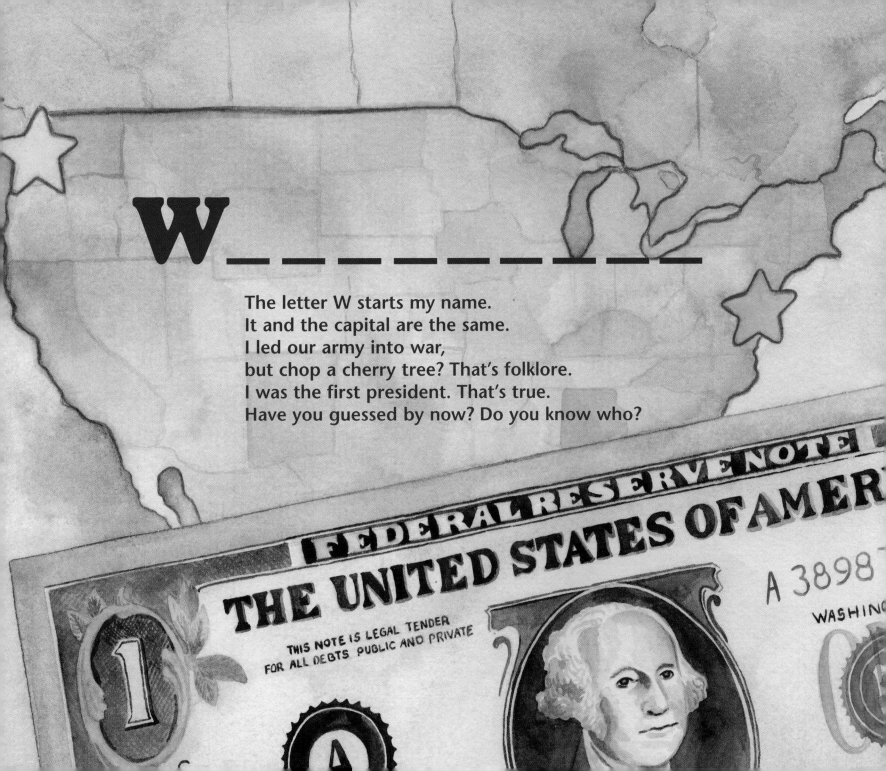

W_____

The letter W starts my name.
It and the capital are the same.
I led our army into war,
but chop a cherry tree? That's folklore.
I was the first president. That's true.
Have you guessed by now? Do you know who?

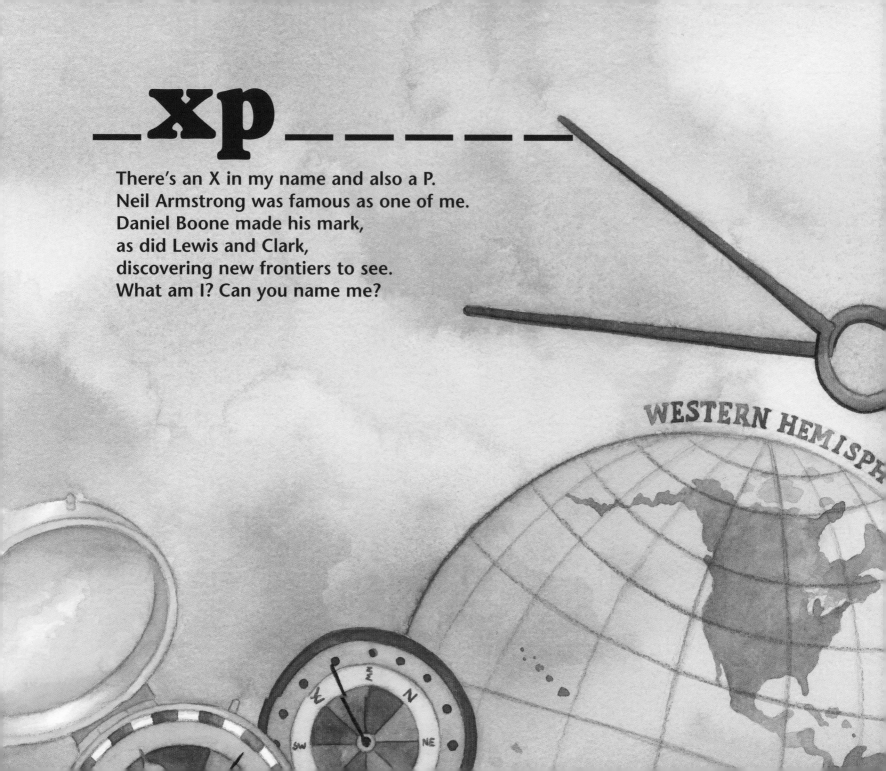

_xp_ _ _ _ _ _

There's an X in my name and also a P.
Neil Armstrong was famous as one of me.
Daniel Boone made his mark,
as did Lewis and Clark,
discovering new frontiers to see.
What am I? Can you name me?

WESTERN HEMISPH

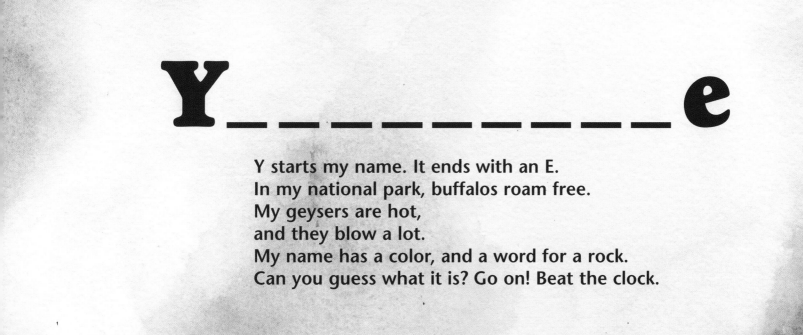

Y_____e

Y starts my name. It ends with an E.
In my national park, buffalos roam free.
My geysers are hot,
and they blow a lot.
My name has a color, and a word for a rock.
Can you guess what it is? Go on! Beat the clock.

Z _ _

My name is a code, it begins with a Z.
I'm a number the post office gives for free
to all the places that receive mail—
a house, a school, even the jail.
I stand for Zone Improvement Plan.
Can you guess my name? I know you can!

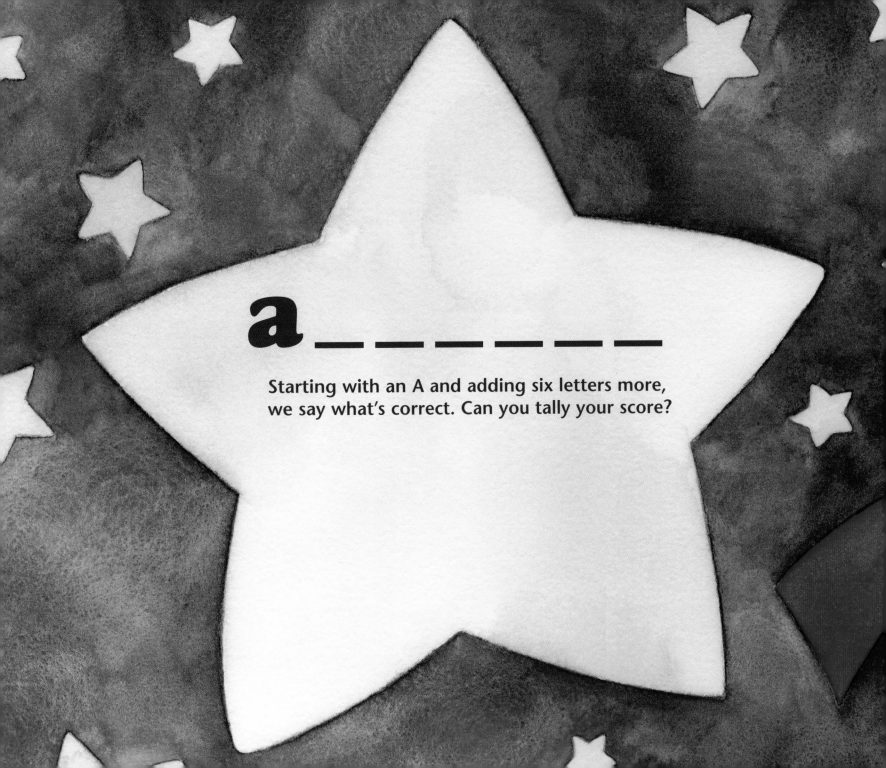

a_ _ _ _ _ _

Starting with an A and adding six letters more,
we say what's correct. Can you tally your score?

apple

baseball

capitol

Disney

eagle

flag

gold

Hawaii

Indians

jazz

King
(Martin Luther King, Jr.)

liberty

military

NASA
(National Aeronautics and
Space Administration)

oil

Pilgrims

Quaker

railroad

slaves

television

united

vote

Washington

explorer

Yellowstone

ZIP
(Zone Improvement Plan)

Ideas for Parents and Teachers

1. If you find one of the riddles tough to guess, look for other clues in the riddle and in the illustration.

2. Think up another clue to add to one of the riddles. Write a couple of lines (a couplet) to personalize the riddle.

3. Create your own illustrations for one of the riddles. Be bold, be colorful, and be careful to not give away the answer!

4. Choose a riddle that you found hard and make it easier or select one that you found easy and make it harder!

5. Make up additional *ABC All-American Riddles.* For example, the letter H could be for Heroes. You could name folk heroes such as Johnny Appleseed and Paul Bunyan. You could mention types of heroes (and heroines) such as sports figures or movies stars and everyday heroes such as firemen, policemen, parents, and teachers, too! Remember to include the letter of the alphabet and, maybe, the number of letters. Look up definitions in the dictionary to make sure you've got the just-right words. Pay attention to your rhythms as well as your rhymes. End each riddle with a question, inviting others to answer your riddle.

6. Share your riddles! You can give them to someone to read or you can perform them in front of others. Another way to share your riddle is to set it to music!

Constructing riddles that rhyme is a wonderful way to explore words and ideas. You'll be surprised how playing with riddles will develop reading, writing, thinking, and presentation skills.

Have Fun!

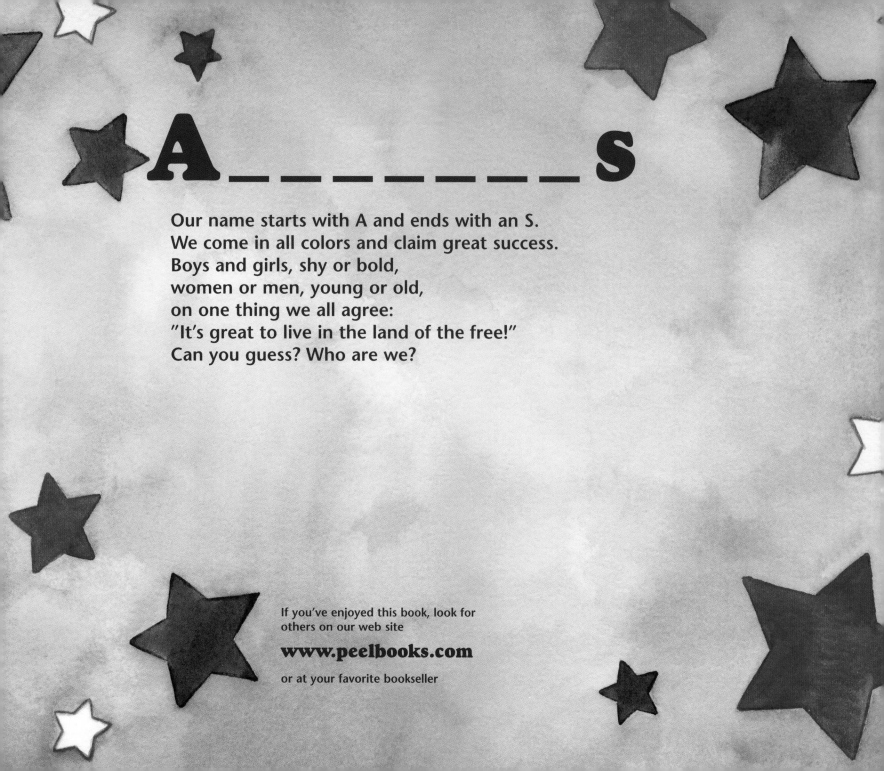

A_____S

Our name starts with A and ends with an S.
We come in all colors and claim great success.
Boys and girls, shy or bold,
women or men, young or old,
on one thing we all agree:
"It's great to live in the land of the free!"
Can you guess? Who are we?